Say What?

*Expressions to Spark Up Your
Conversations and Speeches*

S. Joyce Jones and Margaret Wright

authorHOUSE®

AuthorHouse™
1663 Liberty Drive
Bloomington, IN 47403
www.authorhouse.com
Phone: 1-800-839-8640

First published by AuthorHouse 2/11/2011

ISBN: 978-1-4520-3303-7 (sc)

Printed in the United States of America
Bloomington, Indiana

This book is printed on acid-free paper.

OPINIONS

You can't put a shine on cow chips.

You can't turn something disgusting into something bright and beautiful. Cow chips are what they are.. But some folks say they make a great fire!

Even dirty water can put out a fire.

Speaking of fires, the obvious meaning is that even stagnant or poison water is just as capable of dousing a fire.

Another application is, that even a woman of negotiable virtue can douse a sexual fire in a man. (We didn't say this was a children's book!)

You can fool some of the people some of the time; you can fool some of the people all of the time; but you can't fool all of the people all of the time.

Send this to the politician of your choice.. . or to several.

Every woman marries beneath her.

Wow! Bet you'd get a big argument from a lot of guys about this. Our guess is that this famous columnist really believed that men are hopeless vulgarians. And some of them are.

A wound from a friend is better than a kiss from an enemy.

A friend may unintentionally cause you pain; but an enemy's kiss can kill you. Remember Judas?

Hunger is the best cook.

Aw, yeah Babe! When you're hungry, grits and gravy tastes great even if they're not prepared by Emeril.

To wear like a loose garment.

A loose garment may touch you only on the shoulders, but doesn't bind you anywhere else. This is how you relate to mood-swingers or folks who are just plain obnoxious- - or folks with a short fuse. Their lives touch you very little, so you can afford to be charitable. The expression can mean to hold at arm's length : not letting folk crowd your space. (Must we name names?)

To take her (him) like I find her.

To go along with whatever mood a person is in since you won't have to deal with them for any length of time or on a regular basis. Know a few kiss-offs like this one? They're not all that rare.

A wink is as good as a nod to a blind man.

Don't waste subterfuge on a blind man or someone intentionally blind. The intentionally blind, the emotionally blind, the spiritually blind- - they're unconscious. In any case, the person not paying attention just won't "get it".

Never speak when you can nod, or nod when you can wink.

Great advice from the horse's mouth. No one can play back your words; and nods and winks don't leave a paper trail.

My spirit don't take her. (4)

Another instance where correct grammar would alter the "flavor". (Try saying it correctly. See what we mean?) Conveys the idea that there is something about this person that just doesn't sit right with you. Even your spirit is a hold-out.

Don't play me cheap!

Don't underestimate me. My opinion is relevant.

It is what it is.

Something unchangeable. Calls to mind another expression: you can't make a silk purse out of a sow's ear: it is what it is.

A lie can go around the world while the truth is still strapping on its boots.

It's the awful truth. Some people will believe a lie a whole lot faster than they'll believe the truth. And don't even bother to mix the two: if you do, it'll go over like the Titanic. Ask any politician.

OPINIONS - (con't)

To hold at arm's length.

To avoid a close association with. A person whose friendship you don't want to cultivate. Thankfully, there are not that many to deal with in a lifetime.

Six of one and a half dozen of the other.

Two opinions that mean absolutely the same thing. (It ain't what you say, it's the way you say it.).

Happiness 101.

Some people cause happiness wherever they go; others whenever they leave.

Graveyard love.

This kind of love is not only blind, but deaf and dumb. . .and the antidote is rare. Example: the woman whose husband beats her: this means he really loves her. Yeah, right.

A person who can think on his feet.

Someone quick-witted who can come up with spontaneous and accurate answers.

A toothless lion.

A braggart with no back-up. Someone who can't live up to his roar.

DEFINITIONS

"Tight".

Tight used to mean stingy- -and maybe it still does in some quarters. Also, slightly inebriated. Lately, it meant a close relationship between two people. Today, it means "cool". . .
Whatever. It's your call.

To be "dying on the vine".

Someone not living up to his own potential,; not promoting himself to the fullest; letting talents go to waste. An unmarried person with no prospects.

To "set loose".

There is this story about an African American woman who was asked the reason for her longevity. She replied: "When I works, I works hard. When I plays, I plays hard. But when I sets, I sets 'loose'. Means to remain calm and unflappable.

To outface.

To stare down; to defy or resist. To put up a bold front.

To gross out.

To be offensive. To tell more than anyone needed to know about a bad situation.

To go off half-cocked.

You could get a serious hand injury by firing a gun when it is half-cocked and the bullet cannot clear the chamber. The same is true of telling a half- truth. Trust me: they can be worse than out-and-out lies. There is a sexual connotation to this phrase, but you aren't going to read it here.

Cut me some slack.

Give me a break. A little leeway is needed here.

Cutting the mustard.

Mustard is pungent and tangy as opposed to food that is tasteless and bland. So this saying may mean to put forth a stronger zeal in the effort to define a situation

Talking turkey.

Um-mm, this is a hard one to explain. Turkeys, I am told, are pretty stupid. So if one is "talking turkey" he is breaking the conversation down to the nitty-gritty so that all parties can understand it.

A dim bulb.

A not- so- bright individual. An under- achiever.

A shuckin' and jivin' dude.

Someone who is trifling, insincere. Drop him (her, them) like a bad habit.

Riding bareback.

Sex without a condom.

Eye dialects.

Eye dialects are the deliberate misspelling of words by teens on the internet to save time and to confuse and intimidate old- timers who can (and do) spell correctly.

A woman's ambition

To be weighed and found wanting

Three sheets to the wind.

1. A ship controlled by the elements.
2. A person who is inebriated.

To reap what you sow.

If you sow bountifully, you will reap bountifully; if you sow sparingly, you will reap sparingly. You get out of a project what you put into it.

But never– never, we say – sow stupid.

To lose altitude.

To be overly tired to the point of not being able to relate to the challenge at hand.

When something loses its vitality. . .

1. It is no longer applicable, relevant or productive, like
   a) a job you have quit. . .
   b) an affair that has ended. . .
   c) a project that never got off the ground. . .
   d) A situation that no longer interests you.
   e) a legal fight that wastes the taxpayer's time and money

To cut off your nose to spite your face.

To consent to a worse situation than the original for the purpose of becoming a martyr.

Being a martyr isn't a heck of a lot of fun though, Homey.

Swapping the devil for the witch.

Trading one bad element for another. Truth be told, the devil and the witch are in cahoots.

To pull the wool over someone's eyes.

Can't see through wool, can you? That's the point: to obstruct or prevent someone from seeing something clearly.

To play by ear.

A person who does not read music plays by ear–by hearing a song again and again.

Or, this can refer to a person who does not know what his next move is going to be. He plays a situation 'by ear'. Sometimes it works. Sometimes it falls on its rear.

The pot calling the kettle black.

To be hypocritical. Denouncing something you are guilty of yourself. Happens a lot in politics.

The squeaky wheel gets the grease.

The one who complains is more apt to get attention than the one who goes with the flow.

To cry, with a loaf of bread under your arm.

1. Someone complaining about something when the solution to the problem is within reach.

ANIMAL CONTRASTS

To handle with kid gloves.

Leather gloves are smooth and supple, but kid gloves–from a young goat– are soft and luxurious. To treat someone with care and tenderness.

To sell wolf tickets.

Someone who talks a good fight, but backs off when challenged. Remember the story of the boy who cried "wolf" when there was no wolf around? But when there really was a wolf, no one believed him. The Bush administration was a whole-seller of wolf tickets, only they called them "terrorists".

If you're going to be a bear, be a grizzly.

If you exhibit clout, exhibit the maximum amount in order to survive. Because grizzlies don't back down. Teddy bears are for kids.

If a bird had your brain, he'd fly backwards.

The ultimate put-down. If you are still speaking to your worst enemy, this is probably what you'd say to him.

Don't wrestle in the mud with a pig because you'll both get dirty; only the pig likes it.

A reminder that if you are a mud-slinger, be prepared to get dirty–or find something about mud that appeals to you.

We water our horses from the same trough.

We're alike; we are "drinking buddies". We're on the same page.

I don't have a dog in this fight.

To be neutral. To have no vested interest in a given dispute.

Don't chase a bear with a switch.

We're not really speaking about bears, are we? This expression means that if you are going to go after the powerful, equip yourself; go with all the fire power you can find. Don't go into a dangerous situation unprepared.

Nothing hurts a duck but his bill. (*)

When a duck honks, a hunter knows exactly where he is. By the same token, when we talk too much, we tell more than others need to know about ourselves. Makes us vulnerable.

If you lie down with dogs, you'll get up with fleas.

This is a warning against associating closely with people with contagious reputations- - unless you like fleas.

To have a wasp in your garment.

Something (or someone) is really bugging you. Call Terminix or someone who can handle the situation.

Can't buy a snake a jacket.

A jacket for a snake couldn't cost *that* much; so this expression means that you are broke- - - totally without funds.

As mean as a junkyard dog.

A junkyard dog guards the "treasures" of an entrepreneur who can tolerate no thievery of his goods. Consequently, his junkyard dog is underfed and seriously hostile; so much so that the seller of junk posts a sign that reads: Beware of the dog.

Earwigging.

Earwigging is the attempt to gain influence by persistent debate, or by being a serious demogogue

To beat a dead horse.

An exercise in futility, whether speaking of horses or people.

Never fatten frogs for snakes.

Don't help the bad guys.. Snakes can look after themselves.

You can lead a horse to water, but you can't make him drink.

You can show a strong- willed person what he *ought* to do to survive, but you can't make him do it.

If you can't run with the big dogs, don't go off the porch.

We'll leave it to you as to who the "big dogs" are. But if you can't keep up with them, don't go out and trip over your feet.

To get all the butter out of a duck.

Ducks are greasy. To get all the 'butter' out of a duck is to render it eatable.
To make a situation more palatable by getting rid of its deficiency.

There are no flies on her (him, them).

This expression means that a person is 'fresh'- - in looks and personality. Flies only light on something odorous and rotting.

WISDOM AND TRUTH

A job may be hard by the yard, but a cinch by the inch.

A time factor is involved here. For example: losing weight. It's easy to think: "Oh, I'll never be able to take off *fifty pounds!*" But the wisest choice is not to think of the problem in its entirety. Make yourself satisfied with a *modest* weight loss until the job is done. Trust us: a realistic goal is a lot easier to accomplish than lamenting over the total prospect.

Willful waste makes woeful want.

The operative word here is *willful*. Americans throw away enough food to feed an entire country in Africa., while complaining about how expensive food is.

The man of a few words is the man of the hour.

Someone once said that no one can talk for more than an hour without repeating himself.
And the person who can say it concisely has my vote.

Tact is the art of building a fire under people without making their blood boil.

If you know someone like this, send him to Donald Trump.

Health is better than wealth.

Ask any millionaire with cancer.

If you can't run with the footmen, how will you contend with the horses?

This is from the Scriptures (Jer. 12:5) It means that if you find it difficult to run with other runners, how will you keep up if they were on horses?

Experience is the best teacher.

Our own experience–or someone else's. We don't have to personally experience a situation ourselves to benefit by it.   The old folks used to say you can learn *something* from a fool.

The devil makes work for idle hands.

It's easy for trouble to find you when your hands or your mind are idle. Idleness is the devil's workshop, and he's open for business 24/7..

An idle mind is the devil's workshop.

Not more than a dime's worth of difference between this saying and the one above.
But the mind controls the hands, and perhaps that's the rub.

A drunk man speaks his sober thoughts.

You bet he does! He's too tanked to come up with anything else.

A stumble may prevent a fall.

A small mistake may prevent a greater one. Today, we're so jaded there aren't any small mistakes.

Better to be divided by truth than united by error.

Politics 101 - circa 2010.

If **a** truth divides us, there is always the possibility that at some point we will come together on **the** truth. But if we are united by error, there isn't any hope for us.

We can never be born *enough*.

Being born again is a wonderful experience, but even at that we still sin every day. So we need to be born again every day. That's called *grace, Folks.* (And it's free!))

Where there is no vision, the people perish.

No vision, no safety, no life.

The will of God will never lead you where the grace of God can't keep you.

God leads no one into temptation; but He can keep you from giving in to it if you trust Him.

Work relieves us of three great evils: boredom, vice and want.

Listen, it can't be any plainer than that.

A sermon that is immortal doesn't have to be eternal. (*)

Absolutely. A sermon should be short enough to keep you awake and long enough to keep you aware.

Courage is fear that has said its prayers.

We're all afraid of something: becoming old, penniless, helpless, hopeless Thankfully, prayer gives us courage.

We couldn't climb a mountain if it were smooth.

We have heard a lot about "climbing up the rough side of the mountain", as though this were a difficult thing to do. It may be. But the truth is: The smooth side is impossible to climb.

The key to success is patience.

Can't quarrel with that, but persistence may be a close second.

Those things without repair should be without regard.

The first thing to know about a problem is: can you fix it? If not, forgetaboutit ! Worry causes wrinkles, ulcers and gallstones. (How do we know? Because we're too soon old; too late smart.)

The physical survival of the human race depends on a radical change of the human heart.

This can hardly be any plainer; but it's good advice to everyone who needs counsel.

Example is not the main thing in influencing others; it is the *only* thing.

You may not know it, but someone is always watching you: your children, your family, your co-workers. And some are watching with agendas you may not be aware of..

Not by your roots, or by your toots, but by your fruits.

An enlargement of the expression above. It means that one should not be known for who his parents are; or for what the person *says of himself,* but by his *fruits*- - what he himself accomplishes.

It's not whether you win or lose, but who gets the blame.

With some people, to win is to receive all the glory; but to lose is to blame other people or circumstances. Will we ever become *noble?*

16

Virtue is its own reward.

Don't look for remuneration for a good deed. The good feeling you get from doing the right thing should be reward enough.

We would rather be ruined by praise than saved by criticism.

A condition common to the under-achieved and the unenlightened.

Always try to see yourself through God's eyes.

Oh my! Do we *really* want to do this? Will it discourage us altogether, or make us stronger?

The apple doesn't fall far from the tree.

We used to hear this from our parents as we were growing up: "You gotta be like your Folks." We're like them in appearance, personality, medical make -up, talent and most other ways. The "apples" fall pretty near to the tree with good reason: the gene pool.

You can fool some of the people some of the time; you can fool some of the people all of the time; but you can't fool all of the people all of the time.

Explains itself, but you'll have to make your own application.

Sin multiplies after midnight.

We know that your parents have told you this at one time or another. That's because there isn't much for young people to do after this hour except to have sex. That's because everything legitimate has shut down and the only places open are brothels. Of course, there's the back seat of a car. Trust us- - you're going to repeat this truism to *your* kids one day.

Better to be alone than in bad company.

Aw yeah, Babe. Your own company is preferable to keeping company with a lot of nudniks. At least you are in control of your environment.

Blood will out.

It is certain that the bloodline brings out positive or negative characteristics. DNA is proving that more and more.

Diamond cuts diamond.

Two people who "sparkle" attract each other.

To dig a grave with one's knife and fork.

To over-eat. Research reveals that Americans set the record for obesity. Unless reversed, obesity will kill us.

Necessity is the mother of invention.

When something is needed, someone will invent it. Sometimes a product is invented first, and a need for it is created afterwards. A great example of American know-how and can-do.

Empty vessels make the most noise.

The people who talk the most are the people with nothing creative to say. But you knew that, didn't you?

The love of money is the root of all evil. (1 Tim. 6:10)

Somebody say 'Amen'!

If you don't stand for *something*, you'll fall for *anything*.

Standing for principle is essential, or your opinions will just reflect those of the last person you talked to.

Untaught is better than ill taught.

It is better not to know something for sure, than to be positive about a lie.

Blood is thicker than water.

We are more likely to take sides with our kinfolk than acquaintances and strangers. We just naturally want to see our relatives come out ahead.

Trouble is greater in anticipation than in reality.

Our imagination often runs wild and we suppose that a situation is unfixable. But it turns out that it wasn't as bad as you anticipated. Moral: Be cool and wait for the fog to lift.

Some people don't grow; they just swell.

Growth is the experience, education, progress you can see when you analyze the entire person; swelling only affects the size of the ego.

The poor man's mantra:
Use it all,
Wear it out
make it do
or do without

An egotist:
An "I" specialist.

ACTIONS AND REACTIONS

He who laughs last, laughs longest.

The last laugh usually brings the truth to light and is more enduring. And satisfying.

An ounce of prevention is worth a pound of cure.

Trust us: it's a lot easier to prevent a cold or the flu from happening, than to suffer through it. There's a lot to be said for prevention.

Put your money where your mouth is.

This expression means you are *so* sure of something that you are willing to back up your opinion with a little cash.

To put all your cards on the table.

(. . .Including the one up your sleeve.) Show that you mean to be honest in your dealings with people.

To give the cold shoulder to.

This is almost the same thing as "blowing you off"- - - with a cold wind.

Don't throw water in my mouth!

A saying that originates in Jamaica. It means: don't dilute what I am saying. Tell it like it is.

Your ego is showing.

An ego attack is when you are bent out of shape wondering what people think of you. You wouldn't worry half as much if you knew how seldom they did.

What is your basic maladjustment?

Many times, the real issue isn't the one you are arguing about. The real issue embarrasses us, hurts us, or causes us pain, so we argue about non-essential stuff. But the main thing is to keep the main thing the main thing.

To have all the toys in the sandbox.

This person has everything going for him to make him a success among his peers. Can't do better than that.

Once bitten; twice shy.

The determination not to make the same mistake twice.

Don't p— me off.

You know what this means; and don't pretend you've never said it.

To have a short fuse.

To anger easily; blows up with little provocation. To go from zero to witch in 30 seconds. (We didn't want to be naughty.)

Come here ain't like been there.

Again, toss grammar aside "The present" doesn't have the weight of "been there' (done that) of course. This means to have had a personal experience with an issue.

You can run, but you can't hide.

This phrase was coined by a prize fighter, meaning that there was no place for an opponent to avoid getting hit in the ring.

It can also mean that a person can flee from the havoc he has caused, but it will catch up to him eventually.

What goes around, comes around.

Meaning that what you do today will meet you tomorrow or at some point down the road. But when it comes back to you driven by a hard wind that has picked up mud and debris with it, in-your-face is going to have new meaning.

When things go wrong, don't go with them.

A way of saying that two wrongs won't make a right. Don't pursue a wrong path.

Whose bread I eat is whose song I sing.

Self explanatory: I will love and be loyal to whoever treats me well.

Never burn you bridges behind you.

Don't slam the door behind you so hard that it locks. Be sure that you're not locking yourself out of your own home. It's been done..

It don't work if you don't work it.

Again, the grammar is irrelevant. When you wear that tight, black dress and eyes don't follow you- - you ain't "workin' it.

Professional models - - and other clothes horses- - know how to "work" their clothes to achieve a desired effect. Wear them with a flair; at the same time strutting like it ain't no big thang.

There's many a slip between the cup and the lip.

Don't be so sure that situations will go as planned. The best laid plans of mice and men often go awry. Think about it , Slick.

A miss is as good as a mile.

Long or short range; doesn't matter. If you miss the mark, you miss the mark.

Ignorance is bliss.

An ignorant person has very few worries, hence, a blissful state.

Time is money.

You've heard the expression: timing is everything? Uh-huh. . .Pay your bills late and guess what? There'll be an interest charge on your statement that will be exorbitant for a few measly late days. One of our other expressions applies here: if you can't keep up, you can't catch up.

Cheating is more lucrative than stealing.

It certainly must be because it 's so widespread. We get cheated out of our investments, our entitlements, our jobs, our property, our money and even our identities. Stealing implies intimidation; but cheating is *sub rosa.*. Cheating means that Mr. Slick has come to town and has set up shop. Like the man said, it's getting ugly out there.

SLAVERY AND THE BLACK EXPERIENCE

Section I.

I know his free papers are burned!

When a person of color has "lost his free papers", or when they have been mistakenly burned, he has lost his status as a free man. This was a devastating situation because he was set back into a life of servitude, not having been able to prove his status as a free man. Nor did it matter in some cases whether a man ever owned free papers. Still, we've come a long way, Baby!

You're picking in the wrong row to get your hundred.

Those who picked cotton had to come up with, say, one hundred bags at the end of the day. Because cotton is so light and because some rows were sparse to glean in, a man had to pick his rows carefully to get his hundred. Since cotton is so light, the expression must have meant one hundred bags per month.

Another application is that a person should think along different lines to get his problem solved - - outside the box, perhaps.

If you can't keep up, you can't catch up.

Workers dreaded this designation because it resulted in being put on a harder job than the one they already had; to intimidate them and force them to "toe the line".

A modern day application is that technology is changing so fast that if one doesn't know his way around a computer, it may be difficult to use any of the new technological advances. Are you listening, Grandpa?

Come day, go day, God send Sunday.

A common prayer among field hands who worked from sun up until sundown, six days a week with Sunday being the only day they could rest. Maybe.

You never win freedom permanently. You have to win it time after time. . . whether it's union rights, civil rights or equality for women. You have to keep at it and at it and at it.

Now, ain't that the truth!

Inequality isn't a burden we have to accept, but a challenge to overcome.

Inequality has gone underground, but the challenge to rectify it hasn't. Inequality will be fought tooth and nail until the end of time.

Every good-bye ain't gone.

Don't expect expressions out of the Black experience to be grammatically correct. Never happen. If they are correct, they are flat, like someone singing off key. This is a saying, not of the slavery era, but relevant in the Black experience. . This expression was his assurance that 'goodbye' was not forever, although it proved to be in the time of slavery. It was something positive to say to crying mothers, wives or children.

This expression was used a lot by Afro-Americans during WWII when their units were shipped overseas. It was a playful assurance that he would come back.

Every goodbye ain't gone is also used as a threat, meaning that a person will remember and act on a situation that has not been resolved to his satisfaction. (Look out, Bro!)

Black don't crack.

Putting this in correct English just doesn't do it justice, either. It doesn't have any **pizzaz**. Thankfully, darker skin does not wrinkle easily; but too bad we can't say that about our hair.

What it gon' be like?

Believe it or not, this is a greeting. You can say, 'What is it going to be like?' But saying it in the King's English causes it to lose its flavor. But you'd reply: "I *swear* I can't tell." Or, **Man,_I_ can't make it out!"** (I love our "lingo". Can't beat it for rhythm and color. (No pun intended.) Wonder if white folk have nearly as much fun when they get home and let their hair down (no pun intended.)

One go out; two come home.

A Jamaican expression that means a girl goes out on a date and returns home pregnant.
(Hey Mon, you know it be the truth!) The right response would be: "No way, Mon; this chile too smart for monkey business." If you can't turn down the offer and you're going to sin,
sin smart: don't let this guy ride bareback. If he declines, your response ought to be : "Shove off, Mon; your name has gone abroad."

Man, I'm running on fumes!

So says the person who is barely making it...living from hand to mouth.
Or, so tired that only the fumes left are keeping you going.

Sweet.

A recent expression among Caucasians meaning nice, agreeable, a good bargain, a great break. In the African American community, sweet means "gay". Example: Kevin is really good-looking; too bad he's *sweet.*

Making feet for shoes.

Pregnant. In the Black church, one Sister might nudge her companion, nodding in the direction of a young girl. She'd say, with conviction, "Makin' feet for shoes." And her friend would exclaim "Hush your mouth! How you know?" To which the first woman would reply: "Cause my grandson the daddy."

The color tax.

This is the African American's unauthorized, undocumented personal tax on goods, services, food, insurances, property tax - -including the now defunct poll tax- - I *guess* it's defunct. Whether in the ghetto or on Park Avenue, African Americans *are routinely* over-charged for no other reason than the color of their skin. There may even be a color tax among Hispanics, quien sabe?

Signal Songs

Signal songs are those with a dual message. References to "goin' home" or "goin' to meet Jesus" actually meant that an escape was planned and was about to be executed; a signal to be ready to escape to a better place.

Swing Low, Sweet Chariot...
...comin' for to carry me "home".

Get on Board, Lil' Chillun...
...there's room for many an' more!

Follow the drinking gourd
Follow the Big Dipper.

PROVERBS AND EXPRESSIONS

He who rules must hear and be deaf, see and be blind.

Pretty deep, don't you think? But true. A ruler has to listen to everything, but reject the motives, ambitions, egos in the plan. At the same time, he has to see the advantages but be aware that the end sometimes justifies the means.

If you want good advice, consult an old man.

An old man is like a local library: he has tons of information that is still relevant to the younger generation. Give age and experience a chance.

If erring is inevitable, err on the side of mercy.

We can't get around making mistakes. But if one has to make snap judgments and makes a mistake in doing so, it is better that mercy be the standard of justice. Besides, being merciful helps a person sleep a lot better at night, wouldn't you think?

If reason is not your strong suit, rely on instinct.

Good advice. We can hardly go wrong if we put some stock in instinct. Hey, count the times when instinct saved your life or saved you from a bad scene. But guess what? When we stop relying on instinct, instinct stops happening.

Never trouble trouble till trouble troubles you.

Live one day at a time because tomorrow will have it's own problems.

Love tells us so many things that just aren't true.

Yes siree! That's why they say that love is blind- - and deaf and dumb.

Never draw your sword if a sound blow will do.

This is about overkill, Folks. Don't resort to extreme measures when a good slap upside the head will do.

He is rich who owes nothing.

Aw, Man! Would that we all were all in this group! Will there ever come a time when the mortgage is paid off? (See below)

Ready money works great cures.

Again, we can only imagine- - but hope to win the sweepstakes. (And let the good times roll)

Since the house is on fire, let's warm ourselves.

This is called making the most out of a bad situation. Hey, we have to look on the brighter side, right?

A soft answer turns away wrath.

Difficult to do with in-you-face comments. But try it. Works like a charm.

Vision without action is a day dream; action without vision is a nightmare.

Does "no child left behind" and the war in Iraq come to mind- - in that order?

What must be done at any time will not be done at all.

This is all about procrastination, Readers. We put off non-essential pursuits and end up never doing them at all. But get this: the road to hell is paved with good intentions..

Make hay while the sun shines.

This is similar to the expression above: the sun may not come out tomorrow, so it is better to accomplish a task while the sun is out to ripen the grain.

What the heart thinks, the tongue speaks.

Are you listening, Kramer? Mel Gibson?

Lend money, lose a friend.

Friends remember birthdays, luncheon dates, and your children's names- - but they forget they owe you money. So how smart can it to lend them money?

Any port in a storm.

When you're in trouble, anywhere there is warmth and dryness and TLC is a good place to be.

Brain is better than brawn.

Brawn is okay to get you out of a bad situation, but brain has to give the order.

Different strokes for different folks.

A similar expression could be: to each his own . But the meaning is clear and it is this: "whatever works for you", Babe.

The pen is mightier than the sword.

Words in a book will cut a lot deeper and last a lot longer than a wound by the sword.   Another way of saying, words are power.

You can't make bricks without straw.

The law of substitution does not apply here, Friends. Most situations can't be dealt with by using "something just as good". As the song says: "Ain't nothin' like the real thing, Ba-by".

Sweep in front of your own door.

Don't try to take the sand from your neighbor's eye while you have a beam in your own. Take care of your own business and let your neighbor take care of his.

Give neither advice nor salt until you are asked for it.

Never force an unsolicited opinion on someone. NOTE: This does **not** apply to your children.

The least said, the soonest mended.

If you don't criticize much, you won't have much to be forgiven for.

What the eye doesn't see, the heart doesn't grieve over.

What you don't know won't hurt you.

Distant water won't quench thirst.

When you need answers, you need them now.

A conversation with a wise man is worth a month of study.

A wise man can tell you more than a book can and in less time. (You can tell a wise man by his furrowed brow or by his gnarled hands.)

Perseverance and persistence.

This combination pays off in the long run- - gets results, puts you over the top.

A man is as big as the thing that makes him mad.

If what you **say** angers him , what will he do if you slap his face? Huh?

Bad planning does not constitute an emergency.

Right. It takes a lot of time, effort and "moxie" to undo bad planning. Ex. the wars in Irag & Afghanistan.

Don't be afraid of growing old; be afraid of growing stale.

We like to think of growing old as wearing **well**; and growing stale as wearing **thin**.

By the yard, life is hard; but by the inch, it's a cinch.

This is not rocket science, Folks. If you're going to worry about all the problems you may face for years to come, you're in for a lot of hardship.. But if you take one day at a time it'll be a lot easier on the disposition, the reputation and the blood pressure- - not to mention the pocketbook.

Do not stand in a dangerous place trusting in miracles.

This is called 'presumption'. Expect a miracle when you've done all you can do to ward off danger.

Don't speak unless you can improve on the silence.

This is a soap-box world; everyone has something they feel they must say. And very little of it improves your purse, your appetite or your health.

Don't offer me advice; give me money.

Putting your money where your mouth makes good cents–excuse the pun.

Fish or cut bait.

If all you're doing is drowning worms, ask yourself Dr. Phil's famous question: "How's that working for you? " In other words, if what you are trying to accomplish isn't working, cut your losses and move on.

Goodness shouts; evil whispers.

Everyone is vocal about their good deeds, but quiet about the harm they do.

Gossip needs no carriage.

You got that right! Gossip has its own transportation– wings!

A half-truth is a whole lie.

True, but this saying is often filed under: What You Don't Know Won't Hurt You.
Have you noticed?

Don't think there are no crocodiles because the water is calm.

This is a reminder that things are not always the way they seem. Nothing should be taken at face value- - even if the face is gorgeous.

Every road has two directions.

Yet, how easy it is to choose the wrong one. But wouldn't it be great if there were a pot of gold at either end?

Danger and delight grow on the same stalk.

Don't believe it? Consider the skate board, sky diving, the roller coaster, bungie jumping.

Abundance, like want, ruins many.

Yeah, right. Most of us are familiar with want, but not so much the ruin of abundance.

Advice is least heeded when most needed.

Sounds right if we're talking about our kids.

The best armor is to keep out of range.

Right: hide.

If you're not part of the solution, you're part of the problem.

If you're not making a difference, you're making the disturbance,

Complain to someone who can help you.

Don't go to a gas station to get a loan; go to a bank. On second thought, it might take a loan to keep up with gas prices these days.

Instead of counting sheep, talk with the Shepherd.

This is not only the answer for the sleep problem, but for all others. (You **know** who the Shepherd is, don't you?)

It's not work that kills, it's worry.

Worry, anxiety, stress, depression– - - none of them are fit to live.

We will be known by the tracks we leave behind.

Posterity will judge us by the seeds we scattered and the fruit they yielded.

Don't squat with your spurs on.

If you do, you could get a little behind in your work. (Excuse the pun) A word of caution that could save your hide. Ouch!

When you find yourself in a hole, stop digging.

If the hole is debt; stop spending. If the hole is grief; get counseling. If it's a bad habit, changet your diet, your friends or your environment.

When the chickens come home to roost.

This is to say that you are getting what you deserve - - - that the things you've done have come back to haunt you.

The most dangerous food is the wedding cake.

Aw, not really. In our opinion the most dangerous food is hasty pudding.

Cemeteries are full of people who thought that the world couldn't get along without them.

Alexander the Great, Hitler, Stalin, Tojo, Judas. You can think of a few in this generation, can't you? Some might even be related to you Sorry 'bout that!.

The thought is the father of the deed.

Whatever action you take first begins in the mind. Can you help what you think? Sure you can. Spend some time with the Father (capital F).

The bad workman blames his tools.

"If only I'd had a better education. . more money. . more time. . ."

Free Speech

The right to argue about issues you don't understand.

A revolution is a successful effort to get rid of a bad government and set up a worse one. - Oscar Wilde

Don't use a lot where a little will do.

This has to do with overkill.   A lot of energy spent on a small project is a waste of time, effort and resources.

For age and want, save while you may; for no morning sun lasts a whole day.

Said another way: make hay while the sun shines.

If you can't ride two horses at once, don't join the circus.

If you can't generate some excitement in your field, better look for another occupation.

Men seek less to be instructed than to be applauded.

Instruction doesn't necessarily feed the ego; but applause does it every time.

Never be content with your lot. Try for a lot more.

Great advice. Bigger, better, more of everything; it's the American way.

Old age is ripeless.

If ripeless indicates a time when you will still be agile, in great health, financially solvent, physically attractive, and Denzel Washington wants you for the leading lady in his next flick- - it ain't never gonna happen- - pardon the vernacular.   Neither is old age golden or silver-lined.   Lies, all lies.

Pain is forgotten when there is gain.

You bet your sweet bippy.   A little cash can put some zip in your hip or some pep in your step. Works for me.

Prayer is the key to the day and the lock of the night.

Prayer opens the fortunes of the day and secures them at night

A heavy purse makes a light heart.

Yeah, a heavy purse makes some people light-hearted; it makes others light-headed.

Everyone must row with the oars he has.

Do the best you can with what you have to work with.

A stumble may prevent a fall.

Aren't you glad your "stumble" was just an embarrassment and not a broken hip?

Many a truth is spoken in jest.

Yeah, and it's the saving grace for most comedians, columnists and members of Congress. Otherwise, they'd be facing law suits for slander.

Discretion is the better part of valor.

Good judgment is better than courage or bravery. . it can keep you out of a war.

A good conscience is a soft pillow.

You can sleep well if you've "done the right thing."

A lean agreement is better than a fat lawsuit.

A handshake between not-so-good-friends is better than a lawsuit between not-so-good-friends.

People come to poverty in two ways: accumulating debts and paying them off.

Accumulating debt is the fun part; trying to pay them off makes you feel poor and yucky.

You have to do your own growing no matter how tall your grandfather was.

It's all about character, Homey. You can't rely on heredity when it comes to "measuring up".. Big feet may be genetic, but character isn't..

Whoever gossips to you will gossip about you.

Goes without saying. The need to 'confide' is greater than the need to protect.

Words should be weighed, not counted.

Even a man of a few words should weigh them first.

The person who throws dirt loses ground.

Stands to reason. More specifically, a person loses credibility by introducing thorny topics irrelevant and detrimental to the argument.

An army of sheep led by a lion will defeat an army of lions led by a sheep.

Bold, decisive leadership of the timid will win out over weak leadership of the fearless.

All sins cast long shadows.

We may think that past sins may never come to light, but there are always side-effects lurking in the shadows. ("The shadow knows. . ..")

The afternoon knows what the morning never suspected.

At the end of the day, more is revealed about the life and character than has come to light earlier.

Bad is never good until worse happens.

Right. Consider the price of gas. We are growing to believe that $3.49 a gallon is bad. But when gas prices climb to $4 per gallon- - $3.49 sounds cheap to us.

A handful of patience is worth a bushel of brains.

A little patience may be more helpful sometimes than a whole lot of grey matter.

Leave well enough alone.

If a situation is less than desirable, that's okay. It could be worse if you monkey around with it. .

Always paddle your own canoe.

Deal with your own problems so you can live with the outcome.

Never miss a good chance to shut up.

Advise to people who blurt things out and cause a lot of confusion. Example. " How nice of Ted to look in on you while your husband is away!"

Don't swap horses in the middle of a stream.

... because you could drown or get awfully wet.

Put your money where your mouth is.

If you're **that** sure of something, you should invest a little cash in it.

Practice what you preach.

The old saying "do as I say do, not do as I do" never holds up as well as doing what you **say** you will do. (Got that?)

Republicans will do anything for the poor except get off their backs.

Indeed, Republicans obviously think that the cost of running the country should be the responsibility of the poor- - obviously because they've made so many of them.

I'd rather have them say, "There she goes" than "Here she lies."

Yeah, Babe. Because when they say "Here she lies" - nothing else can be said.

It takes one to know one.

The question is: one **what?** Try thief, liar, flirt, ignoramus, weirdo- -- whatever.

Peace is costly, but is worth the expense.

If peace means negotiating with your enemies, protecting your borders, learning a foreign language, apologizing when you're wrong, sharing your peacetime technology, being a good neighbor- - - then it's worth every nickle.

To scratch each others back.

To have a symbiotic relationship- - one of mutual benefit or dependence.

Taking the bitter with the sweet.

This is what life is all about: including the good stuff with the not-too-good stuff- - and being content.

The receiver is as bad as the thief.

Right. The receiver is keeping the thief in business. Both sound like a 10 -20 in the lock-up to me.

Time heals all wounds.

But it can leave some ugly scars.

Two's company, three's a crowd.

Two's company; three's a detriment to privacy..

Egging the pudding.

To do more or to tell more than is necessary.

We will be known by the tracks we leave behind.

Ask yourself: Will they be big tracks or small tracks? Will they be deep or shallow? Will they go far or stop short of a goal? Will they go through rough territory or stay on pleasant ground. Will they lead up or down? These are the things we need to know about leaving tracks.

Always a pancake; never a waffle.

Never being able to rise to the fullest potential.

When duty fails, age is not far behind.

When you no longer feel committed or responsible, old age is dogging your heels. The elderly are famous for the expression: "Let the kids handle it– they're stronger."

Don't take any wooden nickels.

A caution against accepting something inadequate or worthless.

Never look for sweet juice in half- ripened berries.

If the situation is only moderately profitable, don't expect great dividends.

Putting the pedal to the metal.

Speeding. (Speeding uses a lot more of that precious petrol, Folks.)

Throwing the fat into the fire.

To go whole hog- - beyond what is normally expected.

Can't see for looking.

Sometimes the thing we are looking for is right under our nose, but we it escapes our notice because we are too intent on the search

Gilding the lily.

Putting too much emphasis on something, more than is necessary.

Ignorance is a form of environmental pollution.

A condition that adds nothing positive to the space around an incompetent person so that his environment is enriched in any way.

Silence is golden.

But not when you're speaking to your kids about sex, drugs or porn. And you have to get your hype in **early on.**

Gold is where you find it.

Good fortune - - blessings - - are everywhere. We only need to look down - - or Up.

When spiders get together they can tie up a lion.

An army of little critters can tame a lion

The hand that gives, gathers.

Consider Oprah and other philanthropists. . the more they give, the more they get.

The hand that rocks the cradle rules the world.

Motherhood is still the most queenly responsibility in the world. But its crown is slipping a bit in this generation, what with babies having babies.

People who live in glass houses shouldn't throw stones.

Hey, if your own character is transparent and not too savory, at that, it's not a great idea to belittle someone else.

After three days without reading, talk becomes flavorless.

Correcto. We're all for reading- -books, newspapers, magazines, recipes, the Bible. Hey, talk really is cheap, but stale, if people don't read. Got that, Sarah?

Breaking the ice.

Being able to be first to introduce oneself, open the conversation, or formulate a plan. It breaks the tension among folks who don't know—or like—each other.

Keeping it real.

Telling it like it is- - no frills.

Don't be afraid of growing slowly; be afraid of standing still.

Some people think that pursuing a college degree for four years as growing too slowly. But the alternative is never growing at all.

Failure teaches success.

You may have tried hundreds of things that didn't work, but success comes when you finally find the right element.

Empty vessels make the most noise.

It's a fact: the least intelligent people are the noisiest.

Better to light a candle than curse the darkness.

Better to have a little light, than resort to salty language when you stump your toe in the dark.

Put *that* in your pipe and smoke it!

A caution that the thoughts in your mind are making you delusional. You need to mull over a more productive pipe dream.

You never miss the water till the well runs dry.

You're really going to miss that man (woman) you took for granted for so long. And starting over ain't much fun, either.

First thrive, then wive.

No jive, Clive.

Every man has his own poison.

Sometimes it's a roving eye, a colossal ego, a larcenous heart, or a a drinking problem- - -if he'll admit it.

Every man has a fool up his sleeve.

A bit like the above- - a man who has something he needs to control.

Reckon first and gauge the probabilities later.

Add up the score first, and leave the doubts until tomorrow.

Don't praise the day until evening has come.

The day might begin very well; but then there's the flat tire on the freeway on the way home.

No one is too old to learn *something*.

Unfortunately, there are millions who never read a book without pictures in it, surfed the internet, or looked up something in the dictionary.

Age doesn't protect us from foolishness.

A time-worn expression: There's no fool like and old fool.

Show me who your friends are and I'll tell you who *you* are.

People are known by the company they keep.

How we use our language, intelligence, influence, time and money causes us to sparkle.

A person who speaks well is outstandingly brilliant.

Misfortune comes of itself.

We don't have to do anything in particular for misfortune to come. . . it's a squatter on the farm.

Absence is the mother of disillusion.

If he hasn't come around or phoned lately, Dearie - - he isn't going to. Can't put a smiley face on everything.

A young hunter needs an old dog.

One of you has to be experienced in the hunt, or you'll never trap anything.

Reason lies between the bridle and the spur.

You can guide or you can goad. Guidance is always the best answer.

It's better to stifle a careless remark than lose a friend.

Examples: "Gee, that dress makes you look fatter!" Or, "Is that going to be your summer hair style? Makes you look older." (Shut up, already!)

A man chases a girl until she catches him.

Hey, we don't want to give away all our secrets, but we know when to slow down enough to be caught- - and let him think he did the catching.

Money is the nerve of war.

. . . Or oil, or territory, or water rights. . .

Better an egg in peacetime than an ox in war.

Be more thankful for a snack in peacetime than a feast in war.

Better buy than borrow.

Buying means you've finished the transaction; borrowing means you've got to find a way to pay back.

The first blow does not fell the tree.

Don't quit after the first try when the task is greater than anticipated.

He who asks what he should not, hears what he would not.

When you ask a knotty question, be sure you want to hear a straight answer.

Beggars can't be choosers.

If you're "on a humble" you'll have to take what you can get.

Don't bark unless you can bite.

Can't back up your argument with a stronger one? Then don't even try "selling wolf tickets."

Truth is lost in too much discourse.

This is called filibustering. It always kills legislation in Congress.

It is hard to shave an egg.

Never attempt the impossible.

Forewarned is to be forearmed.

Prepare for the inevitable. Life ain't no bowl of cherries, Mate.

What is sauce for the goose is sauce for the gander.

No favorite is being paid here. Everyone gets the same shot at the title.

Fresh fish and uninvited guests smell when they are three days old.

Plain enough.   Uninvited guests are equally offensive after three days.

Years teach more than books.

Experience teaches more than you can learn from a book.

Trouble brings experience and experience brings wisdom.

Ah, sweet mystery of life, at least I've found you!

Woes unite foes.

A common problem makes enemies friends.

When you're at the end of your rope, tie a knot and hang in there.

There's a knot in the lot of almost everyone because life is precious.

There's always room at the top.

Why? Because climbing to the top isn't everyone's gig- - plus, it makes them dizzy.

Poor by condition, rich by ambition.

Ambition is the wheel that drives the poor.

Counsel is not a command.

No. It's a well-intentioned suggestion.

Delay is the antidote for anger.

If we wait long enough, anger will subside and give way to reason. Works for me!

Who will not be ruled by the rudder may be ruled by the rock.

If you are not guided by principle, you could be headed for the rocks.

Men often make up in wrath what they lack in reason.

Not a good trade-off   Read on

Anger is the management of fools.

That says it all, doesn't it??.

Puberty is manhood running a little wild.

Talk about raging hormones. .   Wonder if parents mention self-control to kids anymore?

Counsel is irksome when the matter is past remedy.

It always makes you mad, doesn't it, when people tell you what you *should* have done?

We'd be a failure but for all the mistakes we've made.

That's what success is made of:: failures. Or the old adage applies; if at first you don't succeed, give it a few more tries.

A word and a stone let go cannot be recalled.

Sometimes our words hurt more than a stone thrown.

Bacchus has drowned more men than Neptune.

More men have "drowned their sorrows" in wine (Bacchus is the Greek god of wine) than have been drowned by Neptune (Roman god of the sea.).

Do good and care not to whom.

Don't be selective with your good works. Anyone should benefit.

Brevity is the soul of wit.

A good speech need not be eternal duration. .

It's easier to flatter a fool than to fight him.

When flattery tells a fool what he thinks of himself, a fight isn't necessary.

God tempers the wind for the shorn lamb.

God protects the helpless from the cold winds—and other catastrophes.

I got it straight from the horse's mouth.

The real story from its source.

Be just before you are generous.

Don't play favorites. Be generous with everyone.

A lad not dry behind the ears.

A boy who has not yet come into manhood and has much to learn. (And it's harder to get his inexperience across to him at this point in time. Verdad?)

It is a sorry house where the cock is silent and the hen does all the crowing.

A condition where the head of the house has lost his marbles and his balls.

Joy and sorrow today and tomorrow.

"Into each life some rain must fall. . ."

Little wit in the head makes much work for the feet.

If you make dumb mistakes, you'd better learn how to distance yourself from them.

Lost time is never regained.

Actually, time is never lost– it's trifled away and you never get it back.

Never look a gift horse in the mouth.

You may not like the gift, but if you say so, you're not likely to get anything else- - ever.

There is none so blind a those who will not see.

Willful blindness; it's a disease without cure.

Possession is nine-tenths of the law.

If you have the article in question and the proof of purchase, though stolen, who's to say it isn't yours?

As effective as a twig in the path of a runaway train.

A self-explanatory but useful adage.

Nothing is given as freely as advice.

And nothing is ignored as freely, either.

To be cut as short as pie crust.

The ultimate put-down, as in: "Shut up and mind your own business!"

Short visits make everlasting friends.

Don't 'camp' when you go over to borrow a cup of sugar.

The best physicians are Dr. Diet, Dr. Quiet and Dr. X.R. Cise

And don't forget Dr. Drink-water!

Take advice to your pillow.

Sleep on it, Sweetie- - and give it at least 48 hours.

There is a black sheep in every flock.

Sure is. One who gets lost, caught in a thicket, and bleats loudly, attracting wolves. And guess what? There's one in every family, too.

To be between a rock and a hard place.

The current saying is to be between Iraq and a hard place. Either way, it's hard to find an exit plan.

To bite off more than you can chew.

Accepting more than one can handle; overloaded.

To cast pearls before swine.

Let's face it; pigs enjoy mud and slop. Pearls would not impress them.

God will make the sun rise with or without the rooster.

The Almighty doesn't have to depend on any person, place or thing to bring about His plans.

No one scratches your hand better than you do.

No other person knows your business like you do.

Fish start smelling from the head.

Dishonesty, graft, fraud, bribery, shady dealings all start at the top.

It's easier to stay ahead than to catch up.

To come up from behind doesn't happen too much among sprinters. You really have to literally run with the footmen.

There is more than one way to skin a cat.

There are many ways to fix a trouble maker; but you can't fix stupid.

The bigger they come, the harder they fall.

Hey, if you ever get in the right punch, your foe will fall like a ton of bricks—and probably be out for the count.

A horse of a different color.

A different situation altogether.

To come a day after the fair.

Arriving too late for the fun: the music, the cotton candy, the hot dogs and the merry-go-round. Sad.

Say What?
MORE DEFINITIONS

The spirit is willing, but the flesh is weak.
The mind has been made up, but courage is lacking.

There is more than one way to skin a cat.
The obvious way to do something is not necessarily the only way.

Uneasy is the head that wears the crown.
Uneasy because of the tremendous burdens of the kingdom. Also, because someone is always out to dethrone the king.

The person who keeps company with wolves will learn to howl.
You will soon imitate your wild companions.

Prosperity makes friends, adversity tries them.
"Friends" that hang around when you are rich will desert you when you go broke.

To have your grits together.
Or your ducks in a row. Whatever.

Every dog has its day. Big dogs have a weekend.
To have the upper hand in the foreseeable future.

To give the devil his due.
Giving credit even when its from an evil source.

Fair exchange is not robbery.
An equal swap leaves no one at a disadvantage.

You can't unring the bell.
What's done cannot be undone.

To make hay while the sun shines.
Work while there is light to see by.

Hunger is the best cook.
When you're hungry any food tastes good.

The straw that broke the camel's back.
The final insult, slap in the face, kick under the bus--is the one that causes the break in a relationship.

The pot calling the kettle black.
One person who has a fault should not criticize another person with the same fault.

A wet blanket.
A person who "throws cold water" on any plan. Or, someone who is not good company.

Washed up.
A has-been. Career is over; ended; finished.

To settle a score.
To get even.

Sitting on one's hands.
To do nothing about a situation; waiting for it to resolve itself.

Uptight.
Tense, nervous.

A tight ship.
Everything is in order. Ex. The admiral runs a tight ship.

A tight rein.
Very little slack. Ex. The nanny kept the toddler on a tight rein.

A tight schedule.

A schedule not permitting much leisure time or unproductive moments.

A tight end..
A football player.

A tight fit.
A shoe or a garment that is too small

A tight weave.
Fabric with a close-knitted design. Or, a hair weave that is pretty strong.

A tight spot.
A pretty serious condition, as when you are down to your last dollar.

Tight money.
When dollars are scarce.   Ex: The government thinks that tight money will stop inflation.

A tight election.
When an election is nose-to-nose ; very close to call.

To be tight.
    1) Drunk, intoxicated; feeling no pain.
    2.) Stingy. Close with money. Ex. Mary is as tight as the bark on a tree.
    3.) (With someone) To have a close friend

To be tight-mouthed.
Not saying very much, Not to be confused with clenched teeth.

To be tight lipped.
Able to keep a secret.

To be tight-fisted.
Another way of saying 'stingy'

Tight discipline.
To be strict, firm, stern, uncompromising.

To tighten one's belt.
To cut your wants down to size. Do with less.

Tightwad.
A stingy person.

A bad workman blames his tools.
A person who always has an excuse for their sloppy work.

Blood is thicker than water.
Family ties are stronger than friendships

When silence is golden.
When saying nothing is the brest response.

A wild goose chase.
An unproductive chase in every direction.

To swallow hook, line and sinker.
To be gullible. To believe something without question.

Taking the leap and building a ladder on the way down.
The leap of faith, believing the outcome will be favorable.

Necessity is the mother of invention.
Problems solved as the result of a continuing need.

At your wits end.
Not knowing what to do next.

To zero in on.
Focusing on the problem. Just the facts, Ma'am.

Money talks.
Sure it does; and most of the time it just says "goodbye".

Between the devil and the deep, blue sea.
No solution in sight; no way out of a situation.

An idle brain is the devil's workshop.
The devil comes to live and reign in a mind without a working plan.

Every cloud has a silver lining.
There's a brighter side to a situation if you wait until the darkness clears.
Cheer up!

One man's meat is another man's poison.
Life has something good for everyone.

You never miss the water till the well runs dry.
We take conditions or people for granted until we don't have them
anymore.

The love of money is the root of all evil.
A fatal attraction for worldly goods makes men devils---greedy ones.

Biting off more than one can chew.
Taking on more than can be handled. An overbite, (excuse the pun.)

An old head on young shoulders.
Someone wise beyond their years.

No strings attached.
No preconceived, prearranged conditions. Free. Gratis.

You're pulling my leg!
You're kidding, right?

Racking your brain.
Trying hard to remember a name, address or telephone number.
(rank, file, serial number, password).

Pressing one's luck.
Expecting too much after the input you've already offered.

A shot in the arm.
1. A reviving , like a pain- relieving drug;
2. a financial benefit.

Under the table. (Sub rosa)
Hush-hush. A pay-off when no one is looking.

Hush money.
Money paid in exchange for a person's silence.

A quick study.
A fast learner.

Keeping a low profile.
Avoiding the limelight; trying not to attract attention to oneself.

Promises are like pie crust--too short or too tough.
Promises, like pie crust have to hold up, don't you think? Piecrust
"makes" the pie. And when it fails the too short-too tough test, it's no
good.

To cut your garment according to your cloth.
To stay within the limits of what you have to work with.

A cut above.
Something, superior, better than the original.

A cut-up.
A clown, or someone who acts like one.

Cut me some slack!
A catch-all. It can mean, Give me a break! I don't believe that! And a lot of other things.

A smack- down.
To tell someone a truth they do not want to hear.

To hit on someone.
Make a pass. Ex: Johnny is hitting on Susan.

To hit it just right.
To get something due you in the nick of time; ie My inheritance comes through the day I retire.

To hit it off.
When two people get along well together

A hit is as good as a miss.
A toss-up. Whatever happens is okay.

Hitting on all eight.
Playing the piano (organ, keyboard) really well. Jammin'.

To get around in.
To know one's territory well. The chef can really get around in the kitchen. (He cooks all kinds of good food..)

To get over.
To know one's craft well. Ex. The actress really gets over with her audience..

To get through it.
To work out one's problem.

To get around it.
To circumvent trouble.

A last ditch effort.
The final try. No mas.

Letting off steam.
Getting something out of your system.
To get something off your chest. To confess; clear the air.

To get hot under the collar.
To become vexed or angry.

To give up.
To surrender.

To give over.
To reluctantly give something you need yourself.

To give in.
To acquiesce.

To give out.
To be tired; fresh out of energy. (A colloquialism: Ex. I'm give out.)

To let off the hook.
To excuse from participation or from blame.

To mind the store.
To take care of business--whatever that may be.

To follow one's mind.
To obey one's first intuition.

Plumb-Nelly.
Someplace off the beaten track. Example: She lives way out in Plumb-Nelly. (A clue that you'll need a map to get there.)

Scratch my back and I'll scratch yours.
Reciprocity. You do something for me and I'll do something for you.

To make from scratch.
To make something from the basics, without the benefit of prior knowledge.

To make ends meet.
When the end of the month and the end of the funds come out even.

A long shot.
Something with a slim-to-none chance of happening.

Right off the bat.
First, immediately.

The right time.
The suitable time, the most appropriate time.

To have one's rights.
Those things guaranteed by the Constitution or some other statute.

Right off the rack.
Clothes that are not custom made to fit the average person. Not like Wilt Chamberlain's, for instance.

Right off.
Not on the spur of the moment. Ex. I can't think of her name, right off. (A colloquialism.)

A rip-off.
Something stolen, cheated out of.

To keep a straight face.
1. Refrain from laughing or showing any other emotion.
2. Keeping an unreadable face.

To keep up with the Joneses.
To try to live within someone else's pay grade that yours cannot match.

To kill time.
To waste time.

To kick back.
Relax, enjoying the scenery or the chance to do nothing for a few minutes.

Discretion is the better part of valor.
Good judgment is the better part of bravery.

One hand washes the other.
It cannot be otherwise. Debunks the adage that the left hand doesn't know what the right one is doing.

A dead-beat.
A person up to no good.

A dead heat.
Two people who finish a race at the same time.

In the dead of winter.
Winter at its coldest.

Dead Silence.
Total, complete, absolute lack of noise.

A dead planet.
Ex. Scientists believe that Mercury is a dead planet.

A dead battery.
1. Inoperative, inactive battery. Car definitely won't start.
2. Someone who is dense, doesn't understand readily.

To stop dead in one's tracks.
To stop abruptly, suddenly

To have a dead personality.
A lackluster, unexciting personality.

A dead ringer.
A look-alike.

To be dead wrong.
Means nothing could be farther from the truth.

A fifth wheel.
Something unnecessary.

A fine-toothed comb.
A careful study or a search. Ex. We researched the subject with a fine-toothed comb.

Strain on a gnat and swallow a camel.
Matt.23:24. To have no difficulty believing something that could happen, but have no problem believing something that absolutely could not happen.

To call a spade a spade.
Refers to something one says frankly, unapologetically.

A lady- killer.
A man women go for in a big way; handsome, intelligent well-to-do, "sharp".

A person who couldn't kill a fly.
A harmless individual.

To kill with kindness.
To be kind to the point of making someone feel ashamed, repentant.

To make a killing.
To receive huge dividends from a venture. Ex. He made a big killing in the stock market.

To kill one's ambition.
To nag a person until he has lost something vital.

To give the cold shoulder to.
The opposite of a warm shoulder to cry on.

A cold day in July.
A reference to something that may never to happen

Till hell freezes over.
A stronger version of the answer above. An event that is never going to occur.

Come hell or high water.
The determination to avoid any major obstacle. Ex: I will not let that happen, come hell or high water.

To hell and back.
A reference to someone who has survived a really bad experience. Ex: She has been to hell and back after two major surgeries.

Not in a month of Sundays.
Something with no possibility of happening.

To fight fire with fire.
To respond in kind.

PROVERBS, SAWS , ADAGES AND QUOTATIONS- - OLD AND NEW.

The fear of the LORD is the beginning of knowledge; but fools despise wisdom and instruction.
    Prov.1:7

Honour the LORD with thy substance and with the first fruits of all thine increase: so shall thy barns be filled with plenty, and thy presses shall burst out with new wine.
    Prov. 3: 8, 10

Charity is no substitute for justice withheld.
    Saint Augustine

A bore is a man who deprives you of solitude without providing you with company.

A bore is a person who puts his feat in his mouth.

Books are sepulchers of thought.

Beginner's luck- A college freshman with an idea.

Peace is our final good.
    St. Augustine

The Bible is a window in this prison- world through which we may look into eternity.

Bigamy is having one wife too many. Monogamy is the same.
    Oscar Wilde

Anger is a condition where the tongue works faster than the mind.
    Queen Elizabeth I

One on God's side is a majority.

Man is the only animal that laughs and has a state legislature.

Man is nature's sole mistake.

G. F. Handel is the greatest composer who ever lived. I uncover my
head and kneel at his grave,
    Ludwig von Beethoven

Failure is a man who has blundered but is not able to cash in on the
experience.

Fame is proof that people are gullible.
    Ralph Waldo Emerson

Bing Crosby-: a man who sounds like everyone thinks they sound in
the shower.
    Dinah Shore

A paradox is an efficiency expert out of a job.

Love: a man's insane desire to become a woman's meal ticket.

An ocean is a body of water occupying about two-thirds of a world made
for man--who has no gills.

Poise is the art of raising the eyebrows instead of the roof.

Tact is the ability to describe others as they see themselves.
    Abraham Lincoln

Obesity is a mental state, a disease brought on by boredom and disappointment.

A taxpayer is a man who has the government on his payroll.

Politics is the art of ignoring the facts.

Poor people are those who expect "no change for the worse".
   - Demetrius

A lame duck is a politician whose goose has been cooked.

Impatience: waiting in a hurry.

Logic is neither a science or an art, but a dodge.

Confidence is the thing that allows you to eat raspberry jam without looking to see if the seeds move.

Seek wisdom, not knowledge. Knowledge is in the past, wisdom is in the future.

It is easy to be brave from a distance.

Cherish youth, but trust old age.

Conscience is the thing that aches when everything else is feeling good.

A conservative is a man too cowardly to fight and too fat to run.

A pickpocket is someone who believes that every crowd has a silver lining.

Juries consist of twelve people of average ignorance.

The wicked flee when no man pursueth.   Prov. 28:1

We are all one tribe spinning through Mother Sky.
Shawnee proverb.

Beliefs are what divide a people. Doubt unites them.
Peter Ustinov

All women marry beneath them.
    - Dorothy Parker

The joy that isn't shared dies young.
    Anne Sexton

A hero is is someone who understands the degree of responsibility that
comes with his freedom.
    -Bob Dylan

An experiment is that which we call sin in others.
    -Ralph Waldo Emerson

Extravagance is anything you buy that is of no earthly use to your
wife.

White men have too many chiefs.
    Nez Perez proverb.

Don't let yesterday use up too much of today.

To retire is to do nothing--and to do it slowly - C.D. Brooks.

Failure is not falling down, but staying down.
    - Mary Pickford

Egotism is self-confidence looking for trouble.

Death is not to be feared as much as an inadequate life.

Education is learning a great deal about how little you know.

How curious that physical courage is so common, but moral courage so rare!
Mark Twain

Life insurance is a plan to keep you poor all your life so you can die rich.

I don't know what the key to success is; but the key to failure is trying to please everybody.   -Bill Cosby

Ingenuity is what you use to get into debt and also what you use to avoid paying it.

No explanation is necessary to one who has faith;   and no explanation is possible to one without faith.   -St. Thomas Aquinas

Irony is jest hidden behind gravity.

Americans are people who trust in God: you can tell by the way they drive.

I'm not young enough to know everything.   -Oscar Wilde

Marry In haste and repent insolvent.

Before you embark on a journey of revenge, dig two graves.   - Confucius

Alimony is the billing without the cooing.

Smooth seas do not make a skillful sailor. - African proverb.

A democracy is a country where you say what you like and do what you're told.

It is no longer good enough to cry peace, we must act peace live peace and live in peace.   -Shenandoah proverb.

Listen or your tongue will make you deaf.

He maketh His sun to rise on the evil and on the good, and sendeth rain on the just and on the unjust. -Matt 5:45

Opera is a musical play written to please the eyes and ears at the expense of the understanding.

The best fruit hangs highest.

Don't strive for success; but rather, strive for value.   -Albert Einstein

A banker is a fellow who lends you his umbrella when the sun is shining, but wants it back when it begins to rain.

Need sells.

Hunger is an instinct placed in man to make sure he will work.

U.S. stands for Unlimited Spending.

Genius is one per cent inspiration and ninety-nine percent perspiration.
   Thomas Alva Edison

Blessed is the man who walketh not in the counsel of the ungodly.
   Psalm 1: 1

Everyone can do *something*. (to help carry the load) -Benjamin Browne

Nat "King" Cole: the best friend a song ever had.   -Jack Benny

I know the meaning of "enough". -Joseph Heller

Mother Nature does not do bailouts.   - Al Gore.

God makes no copies; every person is an original.

Blessed is he that considereth the poor; the LORD will deliver him in time of trouble. -Psalm 41: 1

A friend is like a good bra: hard to find, comfortable, supportive-- always lifts you up, makes you look better, never lets you down or leaves you hanging--and is always close to your heart.

Love is blind. . But not for long.

If two people were just alike, one of them would be unnecessary,
   -T. Marshall Kelly

These six things doth the LORD hate:
A proud look,
A lying tongue,
Hands that shed innocent blood,
An heart that deviseth wicked imaginations,
Feet that be swift in running to mischief,
A false witness that speaketh lies,
And he that soweth discord among brethren.   Prov. 7:16-19, (KJV)

If you never do anything, you never become anybody.

The eleventh commandment : Thou shalt not exaggerate.

To be good, one has to be outraged by evil.

But God commended His love for us in that while we were yet sinners, Christ died for us. -Romans 5:8

We can never be born enough.

A merry heart doeth good like a medicine. - Prov. 17:22

The Christ within you knows the Christ in others.

Advertising agencies consist of eighty-five per cent confusion and fifteen per cent commission. -Fred Allen

The New York Times - the official leak of the State Department. -Mort Sahl

I won't remember the hateful words of my enemies; but I will remember the silence of my friends. -Dr. Martin Luther King, Jr.

A soft answer turneth away wrath. Prov. 15: 1

Some people who give the Lord credit are reluctant to give Him cash.

You haven't begun to live until you feel glad about it.

Common sense is instinct, and enough of it is genius.

An opera is a musical play that pleases the eyes and ears at the expense of the understanding.

God brings men into deep waters, not to drown them, but to cleanse them.

The gem cannot be polished without friction, nor man perfected without trials.
-Ancient Chinese proverb

A beautiful diamond is nothing more than a chunch of coal that made good under pressure.

Strive to drive to arrive alive.
Please Folks, sign the no-texting pledge while driving.

www.ingramcontent.com/pod-product-compliance
Lightning Source LLC
Chambersburg PA
CBHW020352290526
45785CB00005B/2242